Everlasting Grace

Testimonies & Praise

Volume 1

By Regina Johns-Shields

Emerald Jewel Publishing LLC

Everlasting Grace

Copyright © 2026 by Emerald Jewel Publishing

Scripture quotations are taken from the Holy Bible, [Version used, e.g., New King James Version], unless otherwise noted.

Cover design by Regina Shields
Published by Emerald Jewel Publishing
eBook ISBN: 979-8-9928864-7-4
Paperback ISBN: 979-8-9928864-8-1
Hard Cover ISBN: 979-8-9928864-9-8
Printed in the United States of America
First Edition

Acknowledgement

To my Lord and Savior, Jesus Christ— the Author and Finisher of my faith, my Rock, my Redeemer, my Righteous King.

This book, Everlasting Grace, is merely a foretaste… a single drop in the ocean of Your goodness. You have carried me through every valley, lit every dark place, healed what I once believed was broken beyond repair, and loved me back to life, time and time again.

You are the same yesterday, today, and forevermore.
You saw me then. You see me now. And you have already walked into my tomorrow.

How could I not write about you?

It is my deepest prayer that this book will spark a movement of praise—a holy gathering of voices from every corner of the world. May testimonies rise, may poetry flow, and may the hearts of Your people unite to magnify and glorify the only true and living God—Jesus Christ, the King of Kings and Lord of Lords.

Hallelujah.

Forever and always,
Your daughter.

Dedication

In loving memory of our mother, Darlene Johns, whose words live on.

Ma, you were a woman too powerful in God to ever be forgotten. You are still deeply loved and dearly missed. You laughed freely, testified boldly, and lived your faith out loud. Gifted with wisdom beyond your years and heaven-sent discernment, you saw with spiritual eyes and spoke truth with grace. Wherever you went, you never met a stranger—reassuring them, without question, that they were deeply loved by God with an everlasting, agape love.

Through every season of your Christian walk, you pointed hearts back to Christ with conviction, humor, compassion, and unwavering faith. Your words uplifted, your joy was contagious, and your testimonies carried both power and tenderness. You taught by how you lived, and you led by how you loved—genuinely.

Your legacy lives on through the lives you touched and the words you left behind, echoing the truth you stood on all your days: "Only what you do for Christ will last."

Ma, your wisdom still guides us.
Your discernment still covers us.
Your voice still speaks.
And your love still leads others to Him.

With Love Always,
Regina & Cedric

Author's Note

Welcome, Echoes!

I'm Regina Johns-Shields, and it's an honor to share *Everlasting Grace* with you. This book is more than words on a page—it is testimony in motion. Within these pages, you will encounter stories and poetry that lift praise, reflect faith, and point back to the God whose grace never fails.

My prayer is that as you read, you feel His presence meeting you exactly where you are. May these testimonies stir your faith, lift your spirit, and remind you that God still answers prayer.

Thank you for walking this journey with me. Together, we are Echoes— lifting our voices so the world can hear the praises of our mighty God.

When testimonies speak, praises echo.

Blessings,
Regina Johns-Shields

Preface

The world around us is busy, distracting, and restless. Yet in the midst of all that noise, one truth remains unchanging: God is the same yesterday, today, and forevermore. His love is steady. His mercy is constant. His grace is everlasting.

Everlasting Grace was created as a response to that truth. The testimonies shared in this book are drawn from my own life—spanning childhood, young adulthood, and the seasons in between—moments where God revealed Himself as faithful, present, and powerful. These are stories I have shared for years, sometimes met with belief, sometimes with hesitation or doubt, yet I told them all the same. I have never needed universal agreement to speak honestly about what God has done in my life. Writing Everlasting Grace was simply the next step—placing those testimonies in print so they could exist beyond conversation and opinion, standing on their own. This book exists for one purpose above all others: to give God the glory that belongs to Him alone. Belief is personal, shaped by each heart's journey. I can only tell my own story—what God has done for me—and trust it to unfold.

This collection of poems honors the legacy of my late mother, Darlene Johns, whose Christian poetry reflects a life devoted to praise, testimony, and reverence for God. Though she took her heavenly flight in 2013, her voice lives on through her writing—words that uplift, encourage, and point hearts back to Christ.

This book is not about explaining God, but about experiencing Him. To support that journey, I've included Selah Space—dedicated journal pages inviting you to pause, reflect, and rest in what you've received, whether stirred by your own life or by the testimonies within these pages.

My prayer is that Everlasting Grace reminds you of what has always been true: God sees. God hears. God knows. And His grace endures through every season of life.

Introduction

A miracle is more than a moment that leaves us amazed—it is God stepping into the natural with His supernatural authority. It is Heaven interrupting Earth, reminding us that the impossible still bows at His name.

And just as miracles reveal who God is, testimonies reveal what He has done. The two are forever intertwined. A miracle births a testimony, and a testimony keeps the miracle alive. When we share what God has done, we proclaim His faithfulness and hand hope to those who may have forgotten that He still moves.

Miracles, signs, and wonders are not relics of the past. They still unfold in hospitals and homes, in quiet protection and unexpected provision, in moments that felt ordinary until we realized God was there all along. Some miracles arrive wrapped in joy; others come through pain, loss, or survival. Not all of them look like deliverance in real time—some simply sound like, *I made it.*

Testimonies are not polished stories. They are proof of a perfect God moving through imperfect people. Scripture reminds us, "Let the redeemed of the Lord say so" (Psalm 107:2). Every testimony spoken magnifies God's name and strengthens the faith of those who hear it.

Praise is the language of gratitude—the sound of a soul recognizing its Source. It rises in joy and in sorrow, before the breakthrough and after the storm. When we praise, we create space for God's presence to dwell, and our words become worship in motion.

As you read *Everlasting Grace*, pause and reflect. Look back over your own life and ask, *Where did God step in for me?* Because whether your miracle came like thunder or like a quiet breath you didn't expect to take again—it was Him.

That alone is reason enough to testify. Reason enough to write. Reason enough to praise.

"So do not be ashamed of the testimony about our Lord...

He has saved us and called us to a holy life—

Not because of anything we have done but because of His

own purpose and grace."

— 2 Timothy 1:8–9 (NIV)

TABLE OF CONTENTS

Mighty Mice of God

Testimony by Regina Johns-Shields
Miracles Still Happen: A Testimony of God's Divine Provision

Looking back over my life, I can trace the unmistakable hand of God—even in childhood. The Spirit of the Lord lived in our home, not just on Sundays, but in everyday life. That atmosphere was shaped by my mother, a young and devoted believer whose faith never wavered. To my child's heart, she embodied what following Christ looked like—joyful, kind, prayerful, and bold in praise.

Worship wasn't something she did; it was how she lived. People called on her to pray, and she never hesitated—Bible open, faith ready. She raised us with love and discipline, always reminding us, "God sees everything."

One afternoon, around age ten, I was down in our basement on the laundry side hanging clothes on the line with my best friend. The smell of detergent and damp clothes hung in the air. That's when something near the furnace caught our eye. Money. Two old twenty-dollar bills. Forty dollars felt like a fortune in the early '70s

Instead of telling the truth, I told Mama we found it outside. She took us shopping, and I thought I'd gotten away with something. But I had forgotten Mama's warning: *Don't just look left and right—look up. God sees everything. And your sins will find you out.*

"

The next day, after school, I went back into the basement to take the dry clothes down. I turned on the light and froze. Near the furnace again lay three more old twenty-dollar bills. Sixty dollars.

I looked around. Then I looked up. Okay, God… this isn't funny.

I called my little brother down. Three years younger, old soul, already smirking after hearing how I'd found money in the basement the day before, then went back for my dry clothes and found more in the same spot.

"You know the Bible says—"

"Boy, I don't have time for a sermon," I snapped.

He laughed, then said it anyway. "Mama's car is down. She's scared of those mice hopping around in this house out of nowhere, and you know she keeps this house clean. She don't even have money for rat poison—and you out here spending that 'found outside' money."

Conviction hit hard. That night, I told Mama the truth and handed her sixty dollars. She pulled me close and said, "Baby, always tell the truth, no matter what." Then she lifted her hands and shouted, "Thank you, Jesus!"

When I showed her where the money had appeared, she paused. Then she remembered something. Years earlier, a neighbor had mentioned that a clock repairman once lived in the house and kept his workshop in the basement. From that day on, the miracles continued.

For nearly a month, money appeared daily between the furnace and that old workbench—forty to eighty dollars at a time. Bills got paid. The car was fixed. And every afternoon after school, we ran to the basement, wide-eyed with expectation.

Eventually, some family members came with tools to find where the money was coming from. Finally, someone moved the heavy workbench just enough to see behind it. There it was. A narrow ledge—lined with dusty, banded stacks of twenty-dollar bills. We jumped. We held hands. We praised God. Heaven felt close in that little basement.

Mama called a bank attorney whom a relative had referred to her. After looking into it, he told her the money had been abandoned for decades. Because she owned the home, it was legally hers. Ten thousand dollars may not seem like much now, but in the '70s it was life-changing money for a young mother trying to hold her family together, nothing short of God's provision. A miracle reserved for a woman who didn't just attend church— she was the church.

And the mice? Gone. Mama never bought rat poison. She didn't want to kill the mice.

One night at dinner, my brother asked, "Ma, what happened to the mice?"

Mama smiled, lifted her hands, and said, "Their divine assignment was accomplished and completed."

Miracles are real. Provision is real. And yes—God still moves in mysterious, mighty ways.

"Trust in the Lord with all your heart and lean not on your own understanding; in all your ways acknowledge Him, and He will direct your paths."

—Proverbs 3:5–6 (NKJV)

In loving memory of our beautiful mama, Darlene Johns (1941–2013)—

A woman of worship, a vessel of faith, and a living sermon.

Grace Is Knocking at Your Door

By Darlene Johns

Grace knocked at my door one day.
I opened my door, and this is what Grace had to say:
"Hello, how are you today?"
"Okay, I guess." Is what I had to say.

"Who are you, and who are you looking for?"
Grace replied:
"Grace is my name, and I am a part of God.
I am God's love—loving you despite your evil doings.
I am God's forgiveness for all your sins.
I am God's mercy, which He is plenteous in.
I am God's protection, shielding without and within.
I am the sting remover out of death.
I am God's Grace that will keep you from His wrath.
I am the Divine Magnet that keeps the grave from holding you down.
I am Grace—despite your circumstances, I'll turn your frown into a smile.
I am Grace, and that gives you a choice.
I am Grace, who strengthens you in sorrow and makes you rejoice.
I am Grace, who keeps you in this life.
I am Grace—take heed, and listen to godly advice.

Who am I looking for?
Anyone who hears me knock and opens the door.
Grace will come in and enrich your life forevermore.

I am looking for someone whose heart isn't hard.
I am looking for someone who loves God and has a dedicated heart to
Him.
I am looking for someone who knows they are weak—but God is strong.
Someone who willingly admits to God when they're wrong.

I am Grace—
And I am the smile on God's Divine face."

A Place to Hide

By Darlene Johns

In order to survive, everyone needs a place to hide.
Where can you go to truly survive?

A place no one else knows—
To feel secure and serene.
A place where perfect peace sets the scene.

Follow me—
I will show you where love abides, so gentle and fair.
A place forever warm.
A place where there are no more storms,
And no harm will come to anyone.

A place where everyone is welcome to stay—
A place free from foul play.
A place so lovely and light,
A place anyone would long to remain day and night.

A place full of the sun's radiant rays,
A place where love thrives
and deprives no one
Of the serenity and peace that is yours to keep.

How neat it is to know—
There is no defeat where I go.

So, follow me, to Heaven's gates—
Where Love, Peace, and Happiness never escape.

At the End of the Day

By Darlene Johns

You have allowed me to come to the end of another day—
not because of my goodness,
not because I have obeyed—
but because of Your love and mercy.

You guided me through this day.
You used Your rod and staff
to keep my enemies away.

How can I not thank You, Lord,
for Your protective ray?

You have given me this day—my health and strength.
All the day long, you've come to my defense.
You divinely ordered this blessed day.

You sent Your Word
and watched it,
to see that everything went okay.

Now it is time to lie down and sleep—
and I pray, Lord, that You and my soul will meet.

Watch me, Lord,
as I drift into an unconscious world
surrounded by demons and death.

Hide me, Lord,
and take me unto Thyself.

If it is Thy will,
let me awaken to a new day.
But if You decide to keep me—

I would love to stay.

Selah Space

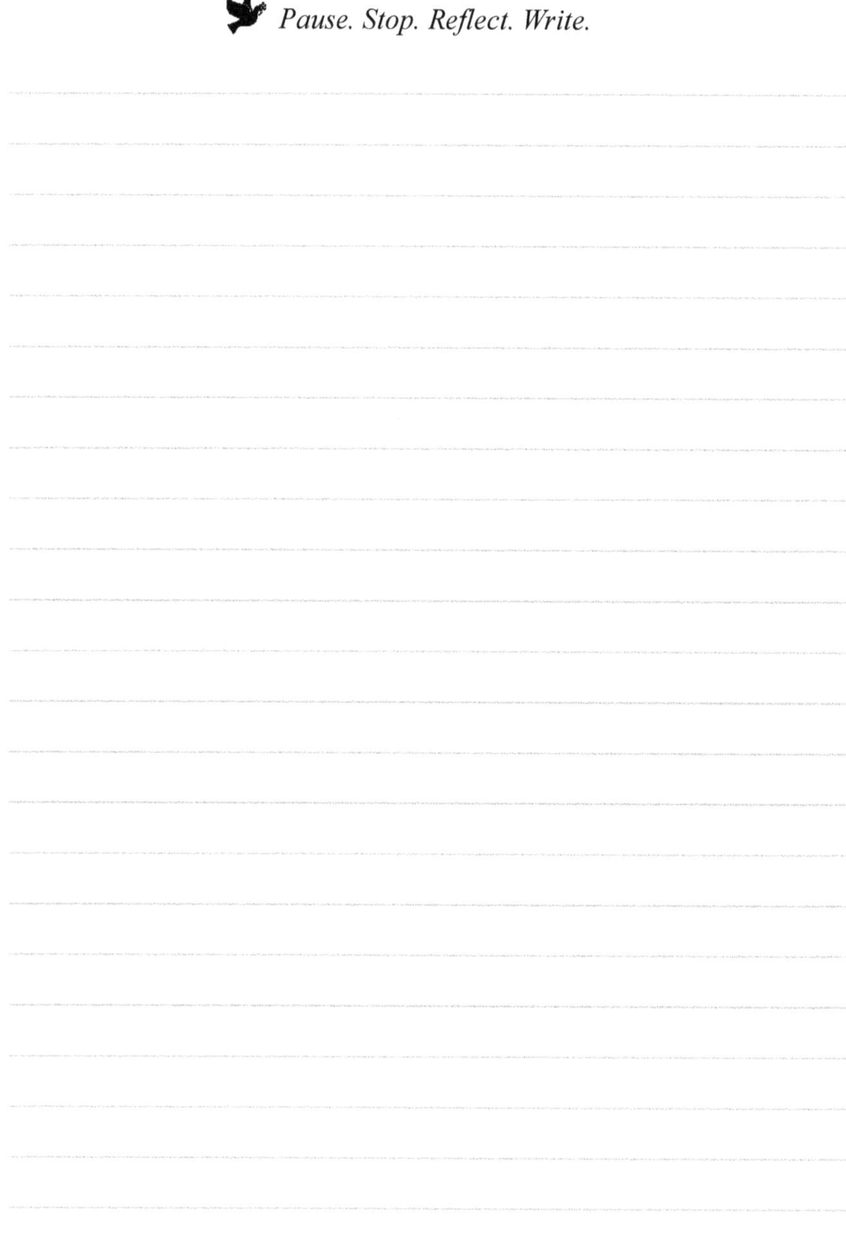

Selah Space

Pause. Stop. Reflect. Write.

Selah Space

Pause. Stop. Reflect. Write.

The Day God Sent Numbers

Testimony by Regina Johns-Shields

It was 1996. I was a thirty-one-year-old mother of four, facing one of the hardest seasons of my life. My husband had been incarcerated, leaving me without an income and fully responsible for our children. We were living in a three-bedroom townhouse in Painesville, Ohio—not far from Cleveland, but far from familiarity—and I was desperate to get back home.

I tried everything. An estate sale. Giving away our dog. Letting go of cherished jewelry. Still, it wasn't enough. The weight of providing for my children while trying to find a way forward felt unbearable. One weekend, as I often did, I took the kids to Cleveland. My boys wanted to play video games at my best friend's house with her son, so I dropped them off and promised to come back before heading home. That left just me and my three-year-old daughter.

I noticed her little face in the rearview mirror sitting in her car seat—
quiet, and sad.
"Hey, Ladybug," I said gently. "Let's stop at Rainbow and get you some new hair bobos."
I didn't have extra money, but I wanted to see her smile.

Inside Rainbow, I let her choose a few colorful bobos and barrettes. As we stood in line, a woman suddenly walked in, her voice cutting through the store.

"Who needs some money?!"

Everyone turned, but no one answered. She stepped farther inside and said it louder.

"I said, "Who needs some money?"

Still, silence.

She continued, "Listen, I've been hitting the number every day. I've been tearing it up. If you need some money, come here."

I hesitated, then stepped out of line, holding my daughter's hand.
"Do you have a pen and something to write on?" she asked.

"Yeah," I said, digging into my purse.

"You play the lottery?"
"Maybe once or twice in my life, but I never hit."

"Well, you're about to," she said. "Write these numbers down. Play the triples straight—can't play them any other way. The others you can play straight or boxed."

She rattled off seven Pick-3 numbers. Some were triples. I wrote them all down.

"When you leave here," she said, pointing to the paper, "go play these numbers. Three doors down is Eagle's Grocery Store. I've been hitting all week. I just wanted to bless somebody today."

"What's your name?" I asked.

"Kim."

"Okay, Kim," I said. "I'll remember that."

After paying for my daughter's things, we went straight to Eagle's Grocery Store. I played the numbers and tucked the tickets and the paper into my purse, not thinking much of it. That night, on our way home, I stopped at a convenience store and sent my son, Spiffy, inside to check the Pick-3.

"Mommy," he said casually when he came back, "the cashier said the number was two-two-two."

My heart dropped. That was one of the numbers.

I walked inside, ticket in hand. "I hit," I told the cashier.

She smiled. "You sure did. You played a dollar on a triple. I can't cash this. We're getting ready to close. Take it back tomorrow to the store you purchased it from.

"How much did I win?" I asked.

"That's one thousand dollars."

I froze. Then I said it—out loud and without shame:

"THANK YOU, JESUS."

The next morning, I drove back to Cleveland to cash it. For the next seven days, I played those same numbers. I hit six out of seven. The only one I missed was the day I left the paper at home and couldn't remember the number—and yes, that one came out too. Still, God made sure I had more than enough. Enough for the move. The deposit. A few months' rent. School clothes. I could even rent the biggest U-Haul truck I could rent. I still had money left over to put in the bank.

It was divine provision in a moment of desperation. At first, I told no one. Not friends. Not even my mama. It felt sacred—something between God and me. Eventually, I did tell her.

"Why didn't you tell me, big head?" Mama laughed.

"I don't know," I laughed back. "It felt like something I had to walk through quietly."

She nodded. "It was only meant for you, baby. To God be the glory."

More than thirty years later, I still think about that miracle. When I share it, some people give me the side-eye—especially because it involves God and the lottery. You know… Christians aren't supposed to gamble. And we're not. But God has a way of showing up through the unexpected.

This scripture always comes to mind:
"Instead, God chose things the world considers foolish to shame those who think they are wise." —1 Corinthians 1:27

God will often use people, situations, or circumstances that others dismiss as foolishness to accomplish His will. We see it all through Scripture— David, a sling, five smooth stones, and one giant named Goliath. No armor. No army. Just God's wisdom over human logic. It's a reminder that He will use whatever He chooses to demonstrate His power, so no one can boast. It's all Him.

Lord, bless the woman named Kim, who fulfilled her assignment that day. And if she has since passed from this life, let that blessing flow through to her family. You used her to bless me—may that blessing ripple through her bloodline.

In Jesus' name,
Amen.

Selah Space

Pause. Stop. Reflect. Write.

Selah Space

Selah Space

Pause. Stop. Reflect. Write.

Selah Space

Pause. Stop. Reflect. Write.

Selah Space

Pause. Stop. Reflect. Write.

Pray for the Man of God

By Darlene Johns

Let us pray for the man of God,
whose heart carries the souls of men.
God has placed upon him the highest commission,
to reach the lost in their sinful condition.

The saints must pray without ceasing,
for God's chosen—that his strength increase.
Pray that daily he's upheld and restored,
equipped to stand and preach the Lord.

Pray for his body, his mind, his defense,
that heaven surrounds him in every sense.

Without the man of God to lead,
we'd wander aimlessly, unaware of our need.
Without his voice, who would proclaim
that Jesus alone saves and redeems our name?

Who would remind us—we are heirs to the throne,
children of promise, never alone?

So, lift up the man of God in prayer,
that he may walk upright, teach, and prepare.
Let him be a vessel—refined and true,
guiding God's people in all they do.

Respect him. Support him. Help him stand.
Let him know we'll obey God's command.
Assure him we'll walk the narrow way,
That faithfulness will mark our day.

It'll make him smile through trials and tears.
To see God's people pressing past fears.
Love him deeply, walk in unity and grace,
And run with him in this holy race.

See God

By Darlene Johns

See God in the clear blue sky,
and always know—He's forever nigh.

See God in the storm and the rain,
in every joy, in every pain.

See God in everything.
See God in the trees,
and worship Him only, please.

See God in the rugged hills—
He'll fight your battles if you keep still.

See God in the deepest sea,
and know He loves both you and me.

See God in the sun and moon;
He is the ruler—coming soon.

See God in man, His sacred image—
for God gave man a part of Himself...
His breath.

You Will Be Known in Heaven!

By Darlene Johns

No one knows your name, you may say,
you're a nobody in this world of prestige.
Everyone is for themselves, fueled by greed.
You've won no popularity contest,
been stepped on and mistreated,
Your protests met with silence or dismissal.

No one has made you feel at home here.
Instead, you feel like a guest.

But child of God—this is not your home!
Jesus has prepared a place for you,
where you will be known.

A place where you'll be expected.
A place where you'll be accepted.
A place of equal opportunity—
a place of peace and unity.

A place of divine bliss.
A place of awesome glory and love.
A place where all the redeemed
have been washed in Jesus' blood.

A place where entrance requires one password—
In Jesus' Name!

So don't fret about this world's sinful condition.
In Heaven, your name will be known.
Documented.
And official.

Selah Space

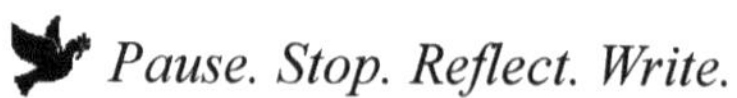 *Pause. Stop. Reflect. Write.*

Selah Space

(Means: A holy pause. A moment to reflect, respond, and rest in what you've just received.)

Selah Space

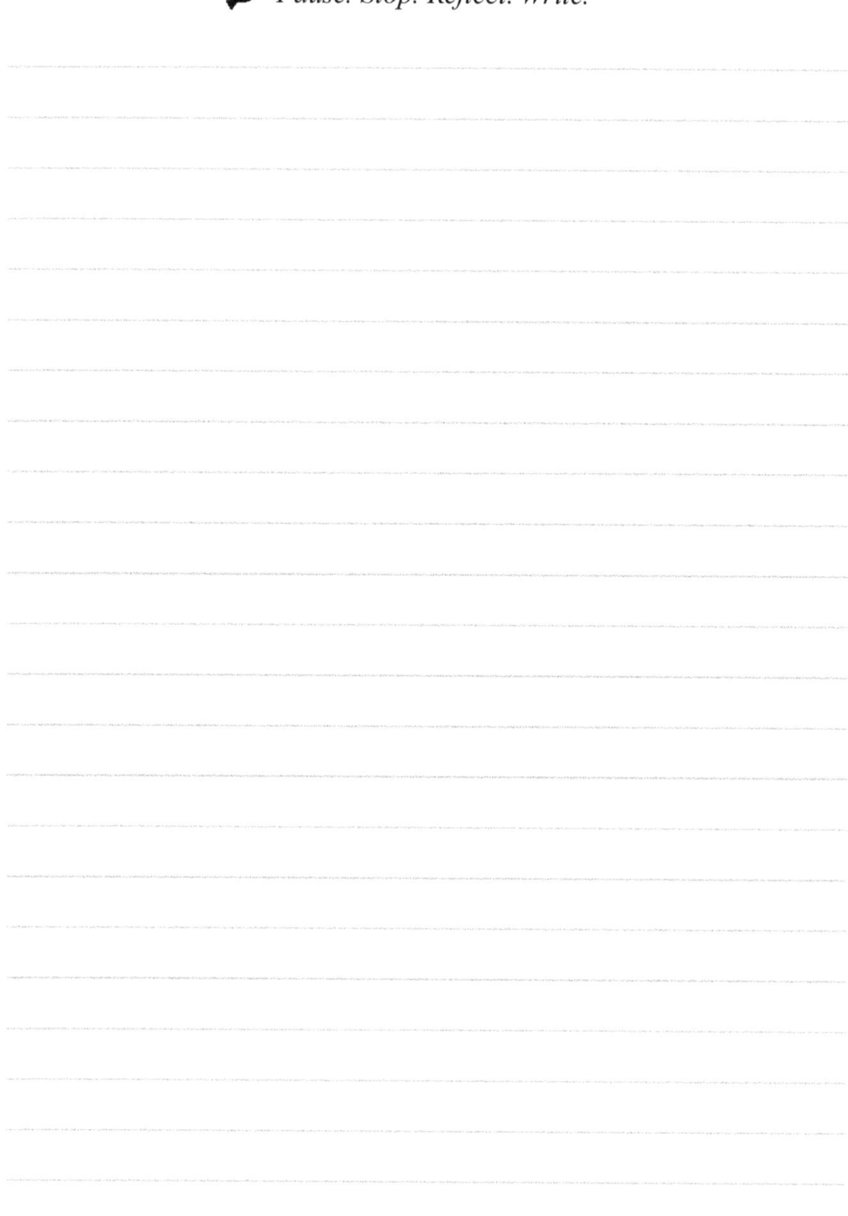

Pause. Stop. Reflect. Write.

Selah Space

Pause. Stop. Reflect. Write.

The $20 Miracle

Testimony by Regina Johns-Shields

It was 1987. I was a young mother, doing my best to provide for two small children. That day, I went to work knowing my baby—still in Pampers—and the supply was running low. Payday was a full week away.

I made calls, hoping to borrow money. Either no one had it, or I couldn't get in touch with those who might. Back then, there was no Zelle, no Apple Pay, no Cash App—just a phone, hope, and prayer. By the time I drove home that evening, the sky had already surrendered to darkness. My heart felt heavy, my thoughts weighed down by worry.

"Lord," I whispered, gripping the steering wheel, "I'm trying to be the best parent I can. I don't have the money to buy Pampers, and he's down to only a few. I can't trust you and worry at the same time. Please—make a way."

Less than a minute from home, my headlights caught something lying still in the middle of the street.

"What's that?" I said out loud as I squinted at the street.

I stopped the car, put it in park, and stepped out. The object was lit clearly by my headlights. I walked over and picked it up.

It was a twenty-dollar bill—folded neatly in half.

Tears filled my eyes as I clutched it.

"Thank You, Jesus," I cried.

I hurried back to my car and drove straight to the store. I bought a large box of Pampers—enough to carry us through past my next payday. That moment taught me something I've never forgotten: God is real. He hears us. He sees our needs. And He meets us right where we are.

It also taught me wisdom—to plan, to prepare, and to make sure I always had more than enough for my children. But most of all, it reminded me that I can always depend on God, as long as I trust Him.

Selah Space

(Means: A holy pause. A moment to reflect, respond, and rest in what you've just received.)

Selah Space

 (Means: A holy pause. A moment to reflect, respond, and rest in what you've just received.)

Selah Space

(Means: A holy pause. A moment to reflect, respond, and rest in what you've just received.)

Selah Space

(Means: A holy pause. A moment to reflect, respond, and rest in what you've just received.)

Look Around and Awake to the Truth

By Darlene Johns

The world is in mourning and grief—
man is looking for a sign of relief.

Sin in the air.
Sin on the streets.
Sin in the homes—
Everyone is crying for peace.

People crying, children dying,
minds are distorted, and babies are being aborted.

Many people have dethroned God.
And excluded Him from their life.
Therefore, without Him,
they have no loving guidance
and Godly advice.

Looking ugly and looking mean,
any excuse to let off steam.
Accusing everyone of their failure—
get mad if you mention prayer.

God has turned them over to a reprobate mind.
The devil is their leader,
and he has them blind.

They believe wrong is right.
They are confused, don't know day from night.
They live insecurely and in fright.
They've been separated from the marvelous light.

God's Word is being proclaimed everywhere;
there is no excuse for man to be in despair.

God's love is in the air that man breathes.
He sent His Son, Jesus, to die for everyone's needs.
His promises are in the Bible—
only if man would read, believe,
and be redeemed.

God careth for you

By Darlene Johns

Many things happen in our lives, and we don't understand why.
But God knows.
And He promises to deliver—He shall never lie!

He is God.
And besides Him, there is none other.

We are His people.
This is His world.
You are a priceless pearl to God.

Being in bondage makes us appreciate being free.
Being cast down makes us appreciate our victories.
When we cry, it makes us appreciate when we can laugh.
Being in pain helps us value our health.
Being poor helps us appreciate our true wealth—*In Jesus*

He is the same God who delivered us in the past.
He is Alpha and Omega—
The First and the Last.

Just remember:
What you're going through shall soon pass.

I Believe

By Darlene Johns

I believe in the sun.
—when it's hidden behind a cloud.
I believe in the wind,
Even when it's not loud.

I believe in moving waters,
Even when it's still.
I believe in the earth,
When it doesn't yield.

I believe in trees,
When they stand dry and bare.
I believe in wheat,
Even when it grows with the tare.

I believe in miracles,
When the doctor has done the best to his ability.
I believe in the power of God—
With all sincerity.

I believe in Jesus,
Whom I have not seen...
I know that He lives—
because my soul,
He has redeemed!

(Means: A holy pause. A moment to reflect, respond, and rest in what you've just received.)

Selah Space

(Means: A holy pause. A moment to reflect, respond, and rest in what you've just received.)

Selah Space

(Means: A holy pause. A moment to reflect, respond, and rest in what you've just received.)

42

Selah Space

43

"A testimony is not an argument; it is an offering. Some will kneel within it. Some will wrestle with it. And some will walk away unsettled. All three responses mean the testimony touched something real.

A testimony is not meant to answer why God did not do something for someone else. It is meant to reveal who God was for you in the storm. God's sovereignty does not mean identical experiences; it means His presence is never absent, even when outcomes differ."

~Regina Johns-Shields

Prepared by the Spirit

By Regina Johns-Shields

December 25, 2019—Christmas Day. As always, our home was filled with love, laughter, and family. Being the mother of four grown children is a blessing, but seeing my seeds—and their seeds—fills me with a joy beyond words.

For this testimony, I will call my second-oldest child by the name we affectionately used—Spiffy. He was the heartbeat of our gatherings. Loving, friendly, funny, and gentle, he had a way of pulling everyone together. Standing 6'3" and weighing about 280 pounds, his stature could seem intimidating to strangers, but the moment you spoke with him, you felt it—there was a grace on him. He never met a stranger. He loved people, and people loved him.

The love and respect he carried for me were immeasurable. Spiffy wasn't much of a texter, but he called me faithfully—two or three times a week— just so I could hear his voice. No one could have told me that Christmas Day would be the last time I saw him.

A week later, as planned, our family gathered for dinner to celebrate the birth of his sixth nephew. Spiffy and I had spoken, and he was supposed to be there. That evening, the house filled with joy as my grandson arrived, carried in by his mother to a chorus of smiles and awe. I asked, almost casually, "Have you talked to Spiffy? He's still coming, right?"

"He is," she said. "But, he said something came up."

Spiffy never made it that night.

As the evening quieted and I cleaned the kitchen, something stirred deep within me. A song rose in my spirit—Reign by William Murphy. Then another—Everlasting God. The songs stayed with me for days. If I woke in the middle of the night, they were still there, and I would sing them softly.

On January 6, 2020, I had a dream.

Jesus and I were walking along a narrow, cobbled street that felt like Jerusalem—ancient, beautiful, and softly lit. The stones beneath us were worn smooth with time, and warm golden light glowed from lanterns along the way.

As we passed one another, He looked at me, and I looked at Him. We were so close I could have reached out and touched Him. His eyes were filled with a love so deep, so knowing that it held me still. There were no words— none were needed. Everything was understood in that look.

Jesus was dressed in white, carrying a lamb over His shoulder. The lamb was not harmed, not bleeding—just sleeping peacefully. Jesus walked in calm authority, unhurried, love radiating from Him as He moved forward. I stopped in the street and turned to watch Him. I stood there for a while, simply watching as He walked away, still holding that lamb, His presence steady and sure.

Then I said aloud, "What was that about?"

I woke up saying it. And when I wasn't singing the songs that stayed with me day and night, I found myself still asking the same question—*What was that about?* I asked that same question for two days.

I called my son. No answer—very unlike him not to answer my calls. I did what I had always done—I prayed. Early Wednesday morning, January 8, 2020, around 2:00 a.m., my daughter knocked on our bedroom door. "The police are here."

At the front door stood three detectives. One asked, "Are you the mother of Spiffy?"

"Yes," I said. "Is he okay?"

"I'm sorry, Ma'am," he said quietly. "Your son was found dead this morning."

The pain was indescribable. Our home collapsed into grief and despair. In that moment, all I could do was call on the name of Jesus, feeling broken and emptied.

Then one of the detectives spoke again. "Ma'am, may we pray with you? I felt the Holy Spirit as soon as we entered your home."

The detectives formed a circle around us and prayed over us—three times that night—between questions, between the crying and wailing, and between what little information they had. After they left, family and friends filled the house. As I spoke with my brother, my memory suddenly returned to the dream.

"That was my dream," I cried. "God was telling me Spiffy is safe with Him."

The Holy Spirit had been preparing me—through song, through peace, through revelation. Even the detective had confirmed it: "I felt the Holy Spirit as soon as we entered your home."

I am eternally grateful to God for that dream. He did not have to do that for me, but He did. And years later, I still declare this as my legacy of faith: not one of my seeds will be lost. We will see Spiffy again.

Yes, losing a child to violence is a tragedy. But the greater tragedy would have been my son leaving this world without knowing Jesus Christ as Lord. He believed. He confessed. And he rests in Him.

Even now, I listen to those songs and find joy—while still shedding tears and missing my son. Reign reminds me, "The Lord is my light and my salvation—whom shall I fear?" And Everlasting God declares, "I will see the goodness of the Lord in the land of the living."

My son will be thirty-two forever. I've told God how that feels. Yet I know He makes no mistakes. My son is safe. And I will see him again. After finishing this testimony, I questioned whether it belonged in this book. Then I opened my Bible, and God answered me:

"He shall feed His flock like a shepherd: He shall gather the lambs with His arm and carry them in His bosom." —Isaiah 40:11

The dream had already told me. His Word simply confirmed it. Spiffy rests in the arms of the Shepherd.

Selah Space

(Means: A holy pause. A moment to reflect, respond, and rest in what you've just received.)

Selah Space

(Means: A holy pause. A moment to reflect, respond, and rest in what you've just received.)

Selah Space

Means: A holy pause. A moment to reflect, respond, and rest in what you've just received.)

Selah Space

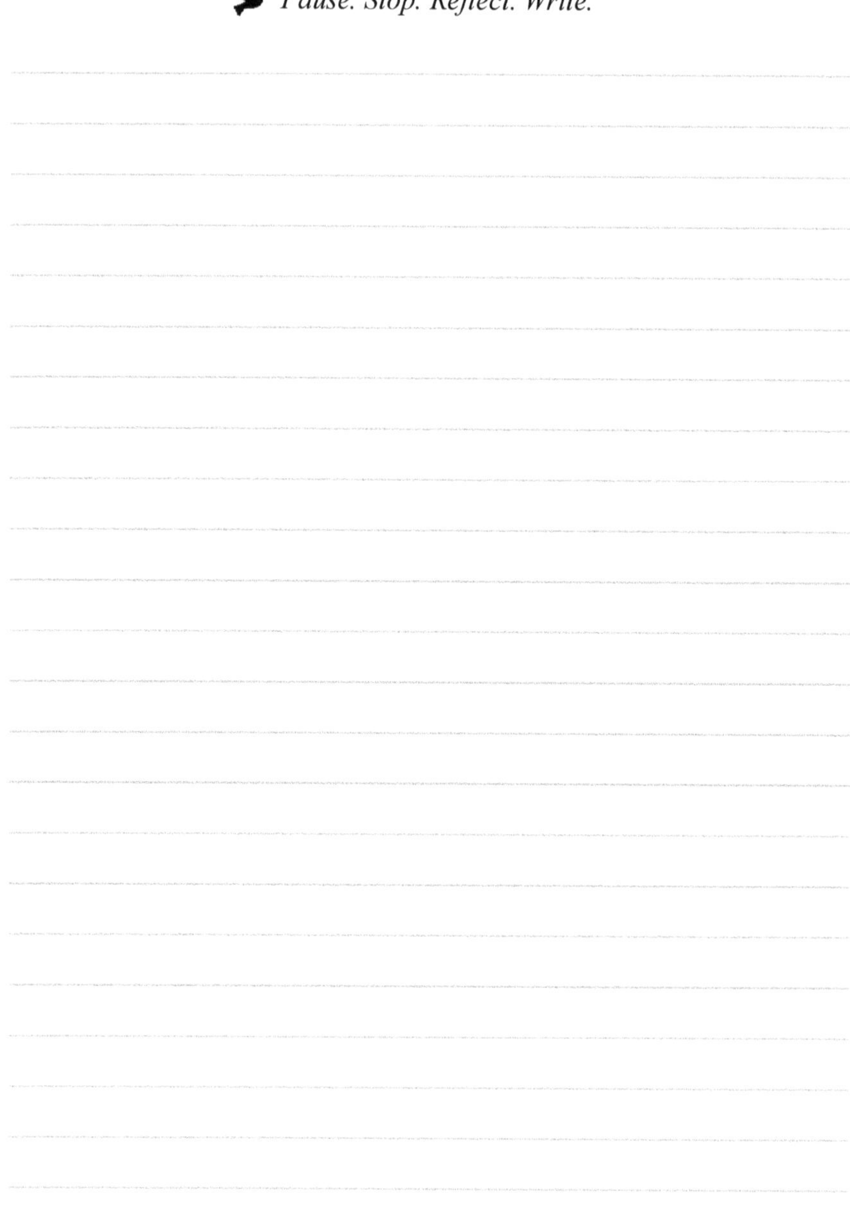

Pause. Stop. Reflect. Write.

Selah Space

Pause. Stop. Reflect. Write.

Who Is the Hope of Glory?

By Darlene Johns

I will not have you grieve like those who have no hope;
The God whom you serve will help you to cope.
Tears the Lord gave—and the right you have to let them flow

For in flowing there is relief;
it will lift you out of a valley low.
You have Jesus, the Hope of Glory—
You know all about His redemption story.

You can cry, it's okay.
He knows you will miss your loved one,
But you will unite again on the Great Day.

Sing All the Way to Victory

By Darlene Johns

As we ascend in our spiritual flight
we must keep a melody of delight.
As we soar upward with all our might,
tired as we fly through the dark, cold nights,
a song of praise will carry us higher.

In our spiritual flight,
the higher we go the louder we must sing—
till we hear joy bells ring.
This melody of joy will give us strength;
we'll be able to nest and have sweet rest.

Never having to fly above our problems again,
for there in heaven sin cannot enter in.
The higher we get, we will be able to see
the crown of victory—
all to God the glory shall be.

The closer we get,
we see it so bright.
We will enter in
if we keep Jesus in sight.

God Send's an Overflow of His Love

By Darlene Johns

God sends an overflow of His Love
When He allows you to awaken to a brand-new day

God sends an overflow of His Love in the oxygen we breathe
And in the Word of God, telling you in JESUS believe

An Overflow of God's Love was on display on Calvary's cross
Where His only begotten Son gave His life for the lost.

Selah Space

Pause. Stop. Reflect. Write.

Selah Space

(Means: A holy pause. A moment to reflect, respond, and rest in what you've just received.)

Selah Space

(Means: A holy pause. A moment to reflect, respond, and rest in what you've just received.)

Never Alone

By Darlene Johns

In the midst of your suffering and pain,
God is pulling the reins,
Letting you know you are never alone.
He is there when everyone else is gone.

In your darkest hour, where no light appears,
God sees your grief,
And His mighty hand catches each tear.
He bottles your tears and mixes them with His love,
To take away the bitterness of your grief
And lift you above.

In acceptance, there is peace—
Accepting God's will helps the grief.
Soon the hurt will cease,
And you will look forward to seeing your loved one.
At God's Resurrection Feast.

Selah Space

Pause. Stop. Reflect. Write.

Selah Space

Pause. Stop. Reflect. Write.

Selah Space

Pause. Stop. Reflect. Write.

Selah Space

Pause. Stop. Reflect. Write.

Held in His Hands

Testimony by Regina Johns-Shields

It was September of 1992 when my husband at the time rushed me to the doctor. Together, we learned that I was pregnant—but the joy was quickly shadowed by concern. I had doubled over with severe abdominal cramps, and soon after, the bleeding began.

At the hospital, the news was grim. I was only a few weeks along and experiencing what they called a "threatened abortion." In plain words, I was at risk of miscarriage, and there was nothing they could do to stop it. The doctors explained gently that either I would lose the baby or the pregnancy might continue—but there were no guarantees. Their best advice was simple: *Go home, rest, and hope for the best.*

But I knew something deeper.
I knew the power of prayer.

I had a praying mama. My mother was a true prayer warrior. Both grandmothers prayed. My aunts prayed. I came from a family that stood on the Word of God. And though I was still young, I had already seen what prayer could do.

Going home with three active little boys was no small task, especially as a stay-at-home mother. But during that season, my then-husband stepped in to help hold things together. The days that followed were difficult, just as the doctors had warned. The cramping and bleeding continued for weeks.

But so did my prayers.

I cried out to God, not with fancy words, but with a mother's heart—pleading for the life of the child He had placed inside me. I trusted Him. I believed He would carry me through to a full-term, healthy baby. And God answered.

He heard my prayers. He heard the prayers of the mothers and grandmothers who stood in the gap for me. He wrapped His hand around my womb and held my baby steady. In June of 1993, I gave birth to a healthy, beautiful baby girl. She is living proof that God is the Keeper of life, a Fulfiller of promises, and a God of mercy and grace.

Hallelujah. To God be all the glory. No matter what doctors say. No matter what the circumstances look like. No matter what we may have done, God has the final word.

He is sovereign. He is mighty. He is faithful. This testimony is not just about my daughter—it is about the love of God. He cares for us, and He especially cares for babies. He knew her before I carried her. He saw her future before I ever felt her kick.

He proved to me once again that He is still the God who hears, who answers, and who holds both mother and child in the palm of His hand. So, I will forever give Him praise. Because when man said, *"There's nothing more we can do,"* God said, *"Watch Me."*

Walk in Your Victory

By Darlene Johns

Walk in your victory, for you've already won.
Whatever you ask of the Lord, believe that it's already done.
Just wait with open arms to receive,
For it is yours because you believe.

Walk in your victory and don't waver.
Know that in you, God has found favor.
He watches His Word, so when there is a need,
His Word is sent to accomplish with divine speed.

So, walk in your victory with your head up high.
What God said He'll do, He will do—
He is not a man that He should lie!

If a Rose Could Speak for Me

By Darlene Johns

The beauty of a rose is pleasing to the eye,
Its fragrance is manufactured in heaven, up in the sky.
A rose's aroma is sweet enough for the bumblebee,
Its vibrant red color represents forgiveness—
Like the blood of Jesus, shed for you and me.

If a rose could speak for me,
It would open up wide and let the beauty of holiness show through.
Nothing shall separate me from the love of my God;
Bowing down low, that I will do
Allowing God's love to fill the gap between you and me.

If my thorns have wounded and offended you,
Please forgive and let us go on in life,
Pleasing God in everything we do—
And live! Live! live!

What Now?

By Darlene Johns

What else can happen? You would say,
Things seem to wax worse day by day.
God allows the devil to do what he may,
Because God knows you won't give up—come what may.

The test seems so hard, and you feel so hurt,
One more thing, and it feels like you're going to burst.
Hang on in there and don't give up,
These hard places are such a bitter cup!

Stand tall like Paul,
Endure to the end—realizing,
Eternal life shall be yours in the end!

Selah Space

Pause. Stop. Reflect. Write.

Selah Space

(Means: A holy pause. A moment to reflect, respond, and rest in what you've just received.)

Selah Space

(Means: A holy pause. A moment to reflect, respond, and rest in what you've just received.)

Selah Space

(Means: *A holy pause. A moment to reflect, respond, and rest in what you've just received.*)

Selah Space

*(Means: A holy pause. A moment to reflect, respond, and rest in what
you've just received.)*

Young and Fearless

Testimony by Regina Johns-Shields

When you're young, giddy, and chasing fun, you don't think about danger or what-ifs. You just move with the night—music loud, laughter louder, never imagining that anything could go wrong. Back then, fear wasn't even a guest at the bar. Little did I know anger and confusion were posted up proudly.

One cold winter night, my cousin and I decided to go barhopping—just two young women out for fun. One of the spots we stopped at was a little place on St. Clair Avenue called The Golden Lady, now torn down and gone for many years. The bar was popular. Small. Alive with music and dancing, packed with weekend noise and laughter.

As soon as we opened the door, there were two empty seats at the bar right in front of the entrance. I complained right away—"I don't like sitting this close to the door or with my back toward the door either," I said, scanning the barroom for another spot. Every other seat was taken. So, under protest, we took off our coats, sat down, and ordered our drinks.

We were bouncing in our seats to the music, laughing, talking, and feeling carefree. The waitress set our drinks in front of us. I lifted mine, took one sip, and that's when everything changed.

At first, it was just a commotion—two men arguing near the back, voices rising, tempers flaring. Chairs scraped. A glass shattered. Someone shouted.

Then came the flashes.

Gunfire.

The sound cracked through that tiny bar like thunder in a closet—sharp, deafening, terrifying. In one motion, my cousin and I ducked down low, snatched our coats, clutched our purses, spun around in our barstools, and bolted out the door. We didn't think—we just moved.

By the time we hit the street, we were breathless. Hearts pounding. Running for our lives back to my car. When we finally slammed the car doors shut, I exhaled hard and, in all my shock and attitude, blurted out, "Damn! We just sat down, and I didn't even get to finish my drink!"

It took me years to realize it was an orchestrated miracle from God.

We walked in, and two seats were waiting—the only ones. We sat down just long enough for His timing to protect us. Just long enough not to be standing when the bullets started flying.

I see it now. Even in my foolishness, God's hand was covering me. Angels were on duty that night—operating in silence, unseen but present. That night could have ended my story. Instead, it became my testimony—a reminder that God's protection doesn't always look like angels in white robes.

Sometimes it looks like two young women sitting in the only seats left. Sometimes it looks like mercy disguised as coincidence.

Looking back, I can still feel that rush of cold air as we ran. Still hear the echo of those gunshots behind us. And now, when I think of that night, I don't remember the fear—I remember the grace.

Because what some call luck was really love. And what I thought were the worst seats was really God's protection.

I'm Not Worthy

By Darlene Johns

I deserve none of God's goodness,
I'm not worthy of His Son's shed blood.
All of my righteousness is as dirty mud.

When I think of God's majestic power,
How he keeps me every hour—
He is my keeper from dangers seen and unseen,
My soul He has redeemed.

I'm not worthy of His love and grace,
His name in my mouth has such a sweet taste.
O taste and see that the Lord is good;
His mercy endures forever.

He has invested in me His Holy Spirit.
To draw those who can't cope,
Encourage others, and give someone hope.

I could never repay Him for all that He's done for me—
He fought all of my battles and gave me.
Many victories!

The Attitude of the Righteous

By Darlene Johns

Blessed is the man who gives to others,
Whether it be time, silver, or gold.

Blessed is the man that receives God's best,
For he shall receive favor and sweet rest.

Blessed is the man who stays with God—
For better or worse, rich or poor—
For he shall be lifted when he has fallen low.

Blessed is the man who obeys God's command,
For he shall inherit the Holy Land.

Blessed is the man whom God has called His friend,
For God shall be with him, even to the end.

Blessed is the man who has been given peace,
For God shall speak the word, and his troubles shall cease.

Blessed is the man who has been through the fire
And came out as pure gold,
For God shall be his strength when he grows old.

Blessed is the man who is scorned and talked about,
For he knows he will have the Victory Shout!

Thank God for Trials & Tribulations

By Darlene Johns

Thank God for your trials and tribulations.
They hurt as you go through,
But when God's divine hand brings you through,
You'll have strength for the next battle, feeling brand new.

If the trials don't come, you would never grow.
If the tribulations don't come,
God's delivering power you would not know.

I thank God for my trials and tribulations, too—
How would I ever know what my God could do?

Through many tears, pain, and fears,
Stumbling and fumbling down through the years,
I was never alone—my God was always near.

The hard places in my life made me acknowledge God.
For His advice;
His grace for me will always suffice.

Selah Space

(Means: A holy pause. A moment to reflect, respond, and rest in what you've just received.)

Selah Space

(Means: A holy pause. A moment to reflect, respond, and rest in what you've just received.)

Selah Space

Pause. Stop. Reflect. Write.

Selah Space

Selah Space

Pause. Stop. Reflect. Write.

Love Teaches Best

Testimony by Regina Johns-Shields

As a mother, I've always believed in teachable moments—conversations that reach deeper than rules, moments that listen as much as they speak, and prayers whispered that your children will truly hear you. I've always preferred to show rather than just tell.

In the 90s, our home was considered a big, two-parent household with four children. I constantly reminded them to be grateful for food, clothing, and shelter—because someone, somewhere, didn't have it. It felt like I said it their entire lives: "Don't be wasteful. Sadly, someone in the world is hungry."

One day, as I prepared dinner, I said to myself, "I need to take my kids to see exactly what I'm talking about. They probably think I'm exaggerating when I say someone doesn't have food, proper clothing, or shelter. I'm tired of sounding like poetry with no meaning. I want them to know that what I say is true."

It was November, one of the coldest months. I took them downtown, to an area where I knew some of the homeless slept on the streets—curled over manhole covers, warming themselves from the rising steam. We bought hats, gloves, socks, and scarves, and I had a few Daily Bread pamphlets to give away. My children at the time were only 5, 9, 11, and 13.

Before we exited the car, I turned to them and said, "I've told ya'll I would never lie to ya'll, so don't lie to me. Now you're going to see why I'm so against being wasteful and being ungrateful—always be thankful. Always remember there are people in the world with less. Don't ever forget you always have enough to share. Come on, let's give them what we have."

As we stepped out, the sight of all the homeless stopped them cold. Men were lying on the frozen ground, huddled in layers of worn clothing and cardboard. The steam from the manholes rose like a soft ghost in the air. My children's faces filled with disbelief and sadness.

When I announced why we were there, the men slowly lined up—humble, quiet. Each of my kids stood with a bag, handing out hats, gloves, socks, and scarves. The men accepted them gently and said, "Thank you," with gratitude in their eyes that spoke louder than words ever could.

When the last bag was empty, we returned to the car. I started the engine and turned the heat up high for my babies. My heart felt heavy, and tears began spilling over as I whispered, "I wish I had more to give."

My then eleven-year-old son spoke up from the back seat, his voice soft but sure.

"Don't cry, Ma," he said. "I know what we can bring them next time!"

Through my tears, I asked, "What baby?"

He smiled widely and said, "We can buy them heaters."

I turned toward him, speechless, grateful for his tender heart. Then I asked, "Where will they plug it up at, baby?"

The car fell quiet.

But in that silence, something holy happened.

My children had seen what compassion looked like. They had felt it. That moment didn't end when we drove away; it settled into them. Love had done what lectures never could.

Empathy was planted that day—in the cold, among strangers, in little hearts that understood more than I could have ever taught with words. That's the power of teachable moments: they don't just shape the child; they humble the parent.

Because when love leads the lesson, it becomes one that both Heaven and Earth remember.

A Reflection of the Testimony: "Love Teaches Best"

My Selah Moment

I need to pause here. Because I'm not just writing a memory—I'm standing in holy overlap: then and now, earth and Heaven, motherhood and loss, love that never left. The child who suggested heaters in that car was my second-oldest son. The same son I lost to gun violence in 2020.

And when I think back on that moment, I realize he didn't just suggest something practical. He revealed who he already was. A heart that thought beyond itself. A compassion that didn't stop at intention. A soul that saw need and immediately asked, *"What can we do next?"*

At the time, I didn't know I was witnessing something prophetic. I thought I was just teaching my children a lesson about gratitude and giving. But God was showing me something deeper—something I wouldn't fully understand until years later.

That moment in the car didn't end when we drove away. It stayed with me. And now, it lives differently. Because love has a way of leaving fingerprints on our lives—marks that don't fade, even when the person we love is no longer physically here.

Looking back now, I understand something I couldn't see then. God allowed me to glimpse my son's heart early. He let me see the tenderness, the empathy, the purity of his spirit—long before I would need that memory to survive his absence.

This is why I believe love teaches best. Yes, there were lectures. Yes, there were warnings. And yes, there were rules. But love was always the foundation. Love is what gave the lectures meaning. Love is what made the warnings protective. Love is what held the rules together. Because God is love. And when love leads, every lesson—spoken or unspoken—has purpose.

Love teaches in moments we don't recognize as holy until much later. Love humbles the parent while shaping the child. And sometimes, love leaves us with memories that ache—yet still glow. This Selah space exists for moments like this.

Moments where you pause, reflect, and allow God to show you what was really happening beneath the surface. Moments where you realize that what felt ordinary was anything but. Moments where Heaven was closer than you knew. So, I sit here now, not broken—but reverent.

Grateful that I was chosen to mother him. Grateful that I heard his voice. Grateful that his love still teaches me. And I wonder—quietly, honestly—how many moments in our own lives carry meaning we haven't yet fully seen. This is my Selah. A pause. A breath. A sacred remembering.

The Simple Things in Life

By Darlene Johns

The simple things in life are the most valuable.
We think less of it because we have so much of it.
The rich think less of his money because there is so much of it.
The people in power think less of it,
Because they feel like they will always be in control.

Oxygen is all around us; it is vital that
We have it to stay alive.
We take it for granted and just believe that it will
Always be there for us to survive.

To see the beauty of the blue sky,
Hear the song of a lark,
Walk to your destiny,
Talk to your Creator,
Taste the flavor of food,
Smell the aroma of coffee being brewed—

These precious jewels are not of your doing,
Yet man takes for granted the mercies of God.
But by His mercy, we are not consumed.

What man calls simple is priceless;
What man counts as valuable is vanity.

Help Me to Give My Best

By Darlene Johns

Teach me to give Your people hope, strength, and might.
Teach me to give Your people spiritual insight.
Teach me to tell Your people to do that which is right.

Give me Your love for the lost, which is so great,
So that I can tell them there is a way of escape—
Warning them to hurry and get into the safety zone before it's too late,
Because we all have an expiration date.

Help me to give my best.
When finals come, I'll pass your test.
From laboring, I'll have sweet rest.

On that great day, I will see
What the Lord has prepared for me.
I can enter in and wait for those to follow.
Whom I've given the gospel bait.

Beloved, Child of God

By Darlene Johns

You are the apple of God's eye, and He is always near.
Whenever you cry out to Him,
He will hear.

He sees your tears, and His heart is touched—
All because He loves you so very much.

He's there to embrace you with His healing wings and His love,
To lift your spirit high and above.

Selah Space

(Means: A holy pause. A moment to reflect, respond, and rest in what you've just received.)

Selah Space

(Means: A holy pause. A moment to reflect, respond, and rest in what you've just received.)

Selah Space

(Means: A holy pause. A moment to reflect, respond, and rest in what you've just received.)

Selah Space

Heavenly Hounds

Testimony by Regina Johns-Shields

It was one of those gorgeous fall days—the sky dressed in blue, the sun sitting just right. The kind of day where the air itself feels touched by God.

My husband and I were heading home on I-90 West, and as we approached the Martin Luther King Jr. Boulevard exit—still "East Boulevard" in my childhood memories—a sudden wave of excitement rose up in me. From the passenger seat, I leaned forward slightly, smiling.

This stretch of road in the fall always takes my breath away. The trees lining the Boulevard stood proud, clothed in robes of fire—vibrant oranges, rich reds, warm yellows—and the ground below them wore a matching blanket. God's artistry was on full display. My husband, knowing how much I loved it, instinctively slowed the car.

He didn't have to ask. He just knew—*let her take it all in. Let her have her moment with God's autumn masterpiece.*

As we exited the freeway and pulled up to the traffic light, we chatted, waiting for it to turn green so I could enjoy the winding road ahead. As soon as the light changed and we started moving, something on the right side of the road caught my eye—right in the middle of me telling my husband how much I loved fall rides through the Boulevard.

I stopped mid-sentence. I gasped. Eight sleek, all-black dogs were arranged in perfect formation beneath a nearly bare tree. Some sat upright—postured, proud, regal. Others lay stretched out, lion-like, with an eerie stillness that didn't quite feel real. They rested on a thick carpet of orange, red, and yellow leaves—so vibrant they looked painted in the afternoon sun.

They weren't alive at all. They were statues.

"Why would someone put those statues there?" I asked. "That's a distraction for drivers coming off the freeway. Somebody could cause an accident looking at that."

We drove by slowly, both of us staring in disbelief. And just as we were passing them, one of the dogs' noses twitched. Just a fraction of an inch. Calculated. Almost robotic.

My husband and I both flinched at the same time and said, "Did that dog just move?"

We looked at each other wide-eyed—then laughed nervously.

"Bae, please turn around," I said. "I need to see if those are real dogs."

He chuckled. "They're not real. But okay, anything for you, Ms. I Need to See."

Now, the Boulevard is a narrow, winding two-lane road, so we had to drive further down, exit to the left, and circle back. It took maybe three minutes.

But by then, my curiosity was fully in charge. And listen—I don't let much pass me. God made me inquisitive *on purpose.*

As we approached the spot again, I rolled my window down to get a closer look. There they were. Same eight dogs. Same black coats. Same eerie stillness. None of them moved. We leaned in, both of us staring—me sticking my head slightly out the window to look closer. And without warning, it was like someone gave a command:

Now.

All eight dogs lunged toward our car at once, barking with fury, bodies exploding into motion, paws tearing through the leaves, teeth flashing. It felt like a scene from a scary movie. But this was very real.

I screamed, "Go, Bae!" as I scrambled to roll my window up, my hands shaking, my heart pounding out of my chest.

We drove off—shaken, laughing nervously, both of us trying to process what we had just seen. What we had almost dismissed. I was still shaking, because Ms. Nosey Rosey did *not* expect those dogs to move, let alone to charge the car. It had felt too still. *Too* still. About a minute later, traffic ahead of us slowed to a crawl.

"Now what happened?" I asked. "We were only gone for about three minutes."

My husband looked ahead. "Whatever it is, we're getting off at the next exit anyway."

But as we crept forward, everything changed. Right there—*right at our exit, where we would have been* had we not turned around—was a mangled mess of metal. A violent head-on collision. One car had crossed the yellow line and slammed into another in our lane. Glass everywhere. Both cars twisted together like two different-colored pieces of paper balled up.

I immediately began to pray for the people involved. As we exited the Boulevard, my husband and I slowly turned and looked at each other. No words were needed. We both knew. Without a shred of doubt—we were supposed to be in that crash.

"Thank you, Lord, for covering us," I whispered.

I believe with every fiber of my soul that God placed those dogs there. And then He told them, "Shhh. Be still." Don't bark. Don't move. Don't chase. Be still like statues. God knew we'd notice. He knew I'd ask. He knew my curiosity would call me back—because He knows me. He knows I'm inquisitive. He knows I'm bold. He knows I need to see things for myself. So, He used my nature for His purpose.

The dogs didn't chase us the first time. Nope. They waited. And when we came back, when the danger had passed—They charged. God gave them permission to *go.* And that charge confirmed the miracle. For me, it was God's way of saying, *Checkmate.* Because He is the Ultimate Chess Player. We rode home in silence after that. No music. No talking. Just awe sitting between us like a third passenger.

Even now, retelling this overwhelms me with gratitude. God's power can't always be explained; it can only be experienced. We've heard the stories.

We know what He can do. But when you live through it? When you see Him move *for you?*

That's when your soul cries out, "Hallelujah," through tears you didn't even know were coming. That's when you know God is real, intentional, and personal. This testimony was too powerful not to share.

One revelation I received that day was this: trust God's timing and instructions—even when they don't make sense. Especially when they don't make sense. Because as Isaiah 55:8-9 reminds us, "For my thoughts are not your thoughts, neither are your ways my ways," declares the Lord.

So, I pray this encourages someone to start looking for God—in the ordinary, in the interruptions, in the strange, in the still. He's always there. In the quiet. In the chaos. In the curve of the road, you almost didn't take. So, when you feel that nudge to pause, turn around, or speak up—*obey it.* God might just be using your curiosity to save your life. Glory to God, forever and ever.

Let the children of God say,
Amen.

"The earth is the Lord's, and everything in it."
~Psalms 24:1(NLT)

It's Time

By Darlene Johns

It's time for the saved and unsaved to get right with God and do it now.
The saved have to stop straddling the fence,
Come all the way over on God's side.
Safety is in the Lord, if in Him we abide.

The unsaved are walking on slippery grounds,
Being out of the ark of safety, they shall fall down.
It's time to believe God and walk pleasing to Him.
Stop wavering in unbelief and sin — we have to flee.

It's time to stop and seek God's face,
Get in His Word; we have no time to waste.
It's time, church, to stop playing;
We must move in the direction of God with haste.

There is no reverence and fear,
Don't believe Jesus' coming is so near.
Refuse to hear what God is saying,
Doing your own thing and not obeying.

It's time to get right, before God's anger kindles and ignites.
It's time to be sincere, for the coming of the Lord is so near.
It's time to open your eyes — the signs are there for us to see.
We have a chance now to escape and to be made free,
By accepting Jesus, who died for you and me.

You Better Not Die

By Darlene Johns

You better not die without accepting Jesus Christ as your Savior.
If you do, you'll lift your eyes up in hell,
Because against Jesus you have rebelled.

You will walk through the valley of death all alone,
In the dark, searching for light,
Mourning and grieving,
Your heart full of fright.

God on the Great White Throne
Awaits you, to sentence you to an everlasting hell,
Where there will be wailing and gnashing of teeth to no avail.

You better not die without accepting Jesus Christ as your Savior.
You'll be tormented continuously,
One way in and no way out,
Locked eternally in the dark —
On you, the beast has placed his mark.

Closing Prayer

Father God,

We thank You for every testimony shared within these pages—every tear remembered, every truth spoken, and every poem of praise lifted. Thank You for meeting each reader exactly where they are and reminding us that Your grace is not fragile, fleeting, or distant. It is everlasting.

Let every word read here stir faith, awaken conviction, and draw hearts closer to You. Where there is weariness, bring rest. Where there is doubt, speak truth. Where hearts have been confronted, let wisdom take root. And where silence has fallen, let praise rise—not as noise, but as surrender.

May these testimonies not end with the turning of the last page. Let them continue—spoken, lived, remembered, and carried forward as living evidence of Your presence and power. Let our lives remain open pages, written by Your hand, marked by obedience, humility, and faith.

We acknowledge You as holy, just, and merciful. We thank You for both the warning and the way of salvation. All honor, all glory, and all thanksgiving belong to You alone.

In the mighty and saving name of Jesus Christ,
Amen.

An Invitation

If you feel led to invite Jesus Christ into your heart as your personal Savior, you are welcome to pray the following prayer. This is a personal decision—one made with sincerity, humility, and free will. God's love never forces; it invites.

Prayer of Salvation

Dear Lord,

I confess that I am a sinner in need of Your grace. I believe that Jesus Christ died for my sins.
and rose again so that I could have eternal life. Today, I surrender my heart to You. Be my Lord, my Savior, and my guide. From this day forward, I choose to live for You. Thank You for loving me, forgiving me, and calling me Your own.

In Jesus' name,
Amen.

If you prayed this prayer with a sincere heart,

Welcome to the Kingdom of God!

"For if you declare with your mouth, 'Jesus is Lord,'
and believe in your heart that God raised Him from the dead,
You will be saved. For it is with your heart that you believe and are justified,
and it is with your mouth that you profess your faith and are saved."
—Romans 10:9–10

The Journey Continues

I truly hope you've enjoyed *Everlasting Grace: Volume 1* as much as I've enjoyed writing and sharing it with you. Every poem and testimony in this collection was born from love, faith, and a desire to remind us that God is still performing miracles every day.

My heart overflows with gratitude and excitement, knowing this is only the beginning. There are many more testimonies yet to be told—and I know this because I still have more of my own. Even more, I know there are stories of grace, faith, and transformation waiting to be shared through *you*.

Your voice matters.
Your testimony has power.
Someone, somewhere, needs to hear what God has done in your life.

If you feel led, I invite you to read the following submission instructions carefully and submit your testimony or poem to be considered for *Everlasting Grace: Volume 2*. Together, we will continue to spread God's light—one story, one testimony, one life at a time.

With gratitude and joy,
Regina Johns-Shields
Publisher | Author | President
Emerald Jewel Publishing

PERMISSION TO PUBLISH FORM (PPF)

Everlasting Grace Testimony & Poetry Submission

I, the undersigned, submit my original testimony and/or Christian poetry for consideration in the *Everlasting Grace* book series.

By signing this form, I confirm the following:

1. I am the original author of the submitted work(s).
2. I grant the owner of Emerald Jewel Publishing permission to edit, publish, print, and distribute my submission(s) in any volume of the *Everlasting Grace* series or related works, worldwide and in all formats.
3. I understand that:
    - My work may be lightly edited for grammar, clarity, or formatting.
    - Testimonies may be condensed for publication if needed without losing my voice or truth.
    - I will not receive financial compensation, royalties, or payment of any kind.
    - I retain ownership of my work and may publish or share it elsewhere.
4. I request that my work be published under (check one):

    ☐ My full legal name _______________________________

    ☐ My pen name: _______________________________

CONTACT INFORMATION

Full Legal Name: _______________________________

Pen Name (if any): _______________________________

Full Mailing Address: _______________________________

City: _______________________ State: ___________________ Zip: __________

Phone: _____________________ Email: _________________________________

TITLE(S) OF SUBMISSION(S):

____

____

Signature: _______________________________ Date: __________________

Send typed submission(s) + this form to:

everlastinggracebook@gmail.com

Submission Checklist – *Everlasting Grace*

Please review carefully before sending your testimony or poetry:

1. Editing & Condensing

   Testimonies may be lightly condensed for publication if needed, but never in a way that alters your voice or the truth of your story. Poems will not be shortened, though light polishing for grammar and clarity may be applied.

2. Typed Submissions Only

   All submissions must be typed and sent as a Word document, PDF, or pasted directly into the body of your email. Handwritten submissions cannot be accepted.

3. Length Guidelines

   You may submit up to one of the following options:
   • one testimony of up to two pages, or
   • up to three separate one-page testimonies

You may also submit up to three poems, each not exceeding one page.

4. Permission Form Required

   Submissions will not be considered without a completed Permission to Publish Form (PPF).

5. Submission Deadline

   All submissions must be received within 30 days of the invitation.

Late submissions may be held for consideration in a future volume.

6. Contact Information

Please include a valid email address, as this will be our primary method of communication. If clarification is needed, you will be contacted by email. Be sure to check your inbox and spam or junk folders.

7. Where to Send

Please email your typed submission(s) and completed Permission to Publish Form to:

everlastinggracebook@gmail.com

About the Author

Regina Johns-Shields is the author and publisher of Everlasting Grace: Testimonies & Praise, a faith-centered collection of testimonies and poetry that honors God's healing power and enduring love. Grounded in reverence, testimony, and lived experience, her writing reflects a deep commitment to glorifying God through real stories of grace, restoration, and hope.

Through Everlasting Grace, Regina creates space for voices that testify, uplift, and give praise, reminding readers that God's grace sustains through every season of life. She writes with humility, purpose, and a heart for testimony, offering words that encourage reflection, strengthen faith, and invite others to recognize God's hand at work in their own lives.

Email us at: **everlastinggracebook@gmail.com**

One Author, Two Voices

You may notice two names connected to my work—Nova Skye and Regina Johns-Shields. They are not two different people, but two distinct writing voices I carry with intention.

As Nova Skye, I write fiction. This is where imagination and storytelling take the lead—most notably in The Sovereign Secret series. These stories explore life, relationships, resilience, and truth through fictional worlds and characters.

As Regina Johns-Shields, I write nonfiction rooted in faith and lived experience. This is the voice behind Everlasting Grace: Testimonies & Praise—a collection of real testimonies, poetry, and reflections that bear witness to God's presence, protection, and enduring grace.

I keep these names separate, not to divide myself, but to honor the reader. Each genre carries a different responsibility, tone, and trust. One invites you into the story. The other invites you into testimony.

Both voices come from the same heart, the same faith, and the same calling—to tell the truth, preserve legacy, and create space for reflection.

Emerald Jewel Publishing Presents

Author Nova Skye
An Emerald Jewel Publishing Author

Emerald Jewel Publishing is home to diverse voices and distinct genres. Readers interested in literary fiction may also explore **The Sovereign Secret: Roots of Resilience** by Nova Skye — an authentic, character-driven novel that explores love, loss, resilience, faith, and personal transformation through an unfiltered, real-world lens.

Discover stories that linger long after the last line.

Available now wherever books are sold.

Emerald Jewel Publishing
"Writing the Past, Present, and Forever."

Book 1 Available Now—
Books 2-7 Coming Soon.

Calling All Authors

Emerald Jewel Publishing Is Open for Submissions

Whether you are a new voice or a seasoned author, your story deserves to be seen and heard. Emerald Jewel Publishing is currently seeking compelling fiction and nonfiction manuscripts that move readers—stories with depth, rhythm, and unforgettable characters and themes that linger long after the final page

Submission Guidelines

• Please submit your first three full chapters for consideration.
• Submissions must be typed and sent as a Word document or PDF.
• Email submissions to: emeraldjewelpublishing@outlook.com
• Use the subject line: "Book Submission – Your Name – Working Title."
• Include a brief author bio, genre, and total word count.

We polish bold voices and timeless stories.
Let your words find their home at **Emerald Jewel Publishing**.

Writing the Past, Present, and Forever.